Rob Thorpe

Knock Knock

*Sin is crouching at the door,
and it's desire is for you.*

Knock Knock
Sin is crouching at the door, and it's desire is for you.
Authored by Rob Thorpe

Published by All In Ministries, Inc.
1 Piedmont Lane
Little Rock, AR 72223

Cover design by Chris Paxton

ISBN: 978-1-7359604-7-0

Printed in the United States of America

Most Scripture taken from the New American Standard Bible

Table *of* Contents

Introduction...5

Preface...7

Chapter 1 - The Primary Theater of Battle 9

Chapter 2 - How Could That Happen 13

Chapter 3 - Think About It..17

Chapter 4 - Open Doors...21

Chapter 5 - Agreements 27

Chapter 6 - The Old Doors...31

Chapter 7 - Existng & Future Doors 37

Chapter 8 - Cleaning Your Mental House.......................41

Chapter 9 - Cleaning Your Physical House.....................49

Chapter 10 - Breaking Agreements.................................53

Chapter 11 - The Great Exchange....................................57

Chapter 12 - Get Up, Keep Running.................................67

Chapter 13 - Developing Your Strategy...........................71

Appendix A - Who Am I in Christ?...................................75

Introduction

We live in a world where spiritual battles often rage unseen, yet their effects are deeply felt—fear, anxiety, shame, addiction, depression, and a persistent sense of struggle, loss, and defeat. Behind most of these struggles lies a subtle but diabolical adversary: Satan, the deceiver, whose mission is to "steal, kill, and destroy" (John 10:10) us individually, our spouse, children and marriage, our mental and physical health, finances, reputation, witness, ministry, and legacy.

But for those who belong to Jesus Christ, the story doesn't end there. Through His death and resurrection, Christ rescued us from the kingdom of darkness, and triumphed over Satan and his earthly kingdom (Colossians 2:15). In addition, Jesus granted all of his followers authority over "**all** the power of the enemy". (Luke 10:19) The question is: Are we walking in that victory and authority?

This book is a call for us to live in the freedom and authority that Jesus paid such a high price for. It is a journey out of oppression into the promises of God—a journey from bondage to freedom, from fear to faith, and from defeat to dominion. Satan may roar like a lion, but he is a disarmed, and defeated foe. Too many believers, however, live unaware of the spiritual war raging against them, and the inheritance of freedom that is theirs in Christ. They settle for less, weighed down by Satan's deception and lies, and remain entangled in the debilitating habit patterns Christ came to free us from.

The good news is this: Scripture does not leave us defenseless. God's Word is filled with truth, power, and promise. It teaches us how to resist the enemy, how to triumph in spiritual warfare, and how to walk in the fullness of our identity as sons and daughters of the King of Kings.

Jesus did not merely come to forgive our sins; He came to "destroy the works of the devil" (1 John 3:8). In Him, we are not just survivors—we are His children, and "more than conquerors" (Romans 8:37). We have been given legal, spiritual and physical authority "over all the power of the evil one" (Luke 10:19).

Satan and his forces relentlessly knock on the *doors* in our mind - seeking to gain entrance, seeking territory, seeking control, seeking destruction. It is here that the battle rages. It is this very field of battle that Paul refers to in Ephesians 6:12, when he says, "we do not wrestle (struggle) against flesh and blood but against principalities, against powers, against the rulers of the darkness of this world".

Satan's ongoing campaign of lies, deception, doubt, guilt, shame, condemnation, insecurity, anxiety, fear, depression, and dozens more is meant to wear us down, steal our joy, and render us ultimately joyless, hopeless, and powerless as believers.

We must know - and remember daily - the only power Satan has over us is the power we grant him.

If, like Eve, we listen to his lies, and give thought to his deception - we will open a doorway into our heart/mind by agreeing with his deceit, and give him permission to begin building a stronghold in our life. He will take each and every such opportunity (we grant him) to establish territory/space in our mind that will then affect our thoughts, actions, and ultimately our life. His ultimate goal is to "devour" (*destroy completely - Gr.*) every believer.

We must be constantly vigilant to "take our thoughts captive" (2 Corinthians 10:5), reject every lie of the enemy, and keep strongholds from ever being established.

We must also take the time to utilize the "divinely powerful weapons" (2 Corinthians 10:4) we have been given as God's children, and completely demolish any existing strongholds we have allowed to stand in our lives for years.

Let's shut all open doors - then grab our spiritual sledgehammer and start swinging away at any strongholds!

Enough is enough!

"To stay free, people need to know: (1) who they are in Christ, (2) the authority, weapons, and protection of the believer, (3) the nature of the battle that is going on in their minds, and (4) how to walk by faith by the power of the Holy Spirit according to what God says is true."

Neil Anderson

Preface

Satan wasn't always the enemy. The Bible teaches that God created him as a stunningly beautiful and powerful angel. He was likely the highest of all angels, described as the "anointed cherub" and "full of wisdom and beauty". He walked in God's very presence on the "holy mount of God" and was "blameless in all his ways". But pride got the best of him. He wasn't content with his high status, but wanted to be God, not serve God. This desire led to his rebellion. Because of his pride and ambition, God cast him out of heaven and down to earth as his temporary dwelling place. See (Isaiah 14:12-15; Ezekiel 28:12-17)

The Bible gives Satan many names, including: " the devil" (Matthew 4:1-11); "the adversary" (1 Peter 5:8); "the accuser,"(Revelation 12:10); "the evil one," (1 John 5:18-19); "a liar and the father of lies," (John 8:44); "an angel of light" (2 Corinthians 11:14); "a roaring lion seeking whom he may devour" (1 Peter 5:8); and "the ruler of this world"(John 12:31); "the prince of the power of the air" (Ephesians 2:2), and even "the god of this world" (2 Corinthians 2:2). He is not just a symbol of evil—he is an actual being with great intelligence, cunning and power, but he is not equal to God.

Satan is not the opposite of God. He was created by God and is subject to God. He is NOT omnipresent, omnipotent, or omniscient. He is NOT everywhere all the time, or have unlimited power, NOR can he know your thoughts. He is an angel.

Powerful indeed, but still an angel.

Demons, too, are angels. They were also created by God, but chose to join Satan in his rebellion against God. When Satan fell and was cast down to earth, he convinced one third of the heavenly angels to follow him. These fallen angels became what we call demons (Revelation 12:4, 9). Some are already locked away (2 Peter 2:4), but most are still active, working under Satan's command. These fallen angels, corrupted by their disobedience and rebellion, are also described as "evil spirits,"(Luke 7:21, Acts 19:12) "unclean or foul spirits,"(Mark 1:34, 9:25, Luke 4:41) "principalities, powers, rulers of the darkness of this world", (Ephesians 6:12, Romans 8:38, Colossians 2:15). Since getting kicked out of heaven and cast down to earth, Satan and his forces have focused on one primary agenda, one battle plan - destroy the glory and plan of God and His people.

Revelation, Chapter 12, offers a reference in verse 17:

> *" Then the dragon became furious with the woman and went off to make war on the rest of his offspring, on those who keep the commandments of God and hold to the testimony of Jesus ".*

If you claim to be a follower/believer in Jesus Christ - that means YOU.

You and I were born into a world at war. Unlike an earthly war, this war is fought in the spiritual realm. There will be no truce, no prisoner exchange, and no cease-fire. This is a battle to the death. These men said it well:

> *"We are locked in a battle. This is not a friendly, gentlemen's discussion. It is a life and death conflict between the spiritual hosts of wickedness and those who claim the name of Christ ".*
> *— Frances Schaeffer*

> *It doesn't matter whether you want to be in a spiritual battle; you are in one. The battle is between good and evil, and you are the prize.*
> *— Charles Stanley*

> *Life is war. That's not all it is. But it is always that. Our weakness in prayer is owing largely to our neglect of this truth.*
> *— John Piper*

Once you realize that you wake each morning in a war zone, the many Bible verses referencing "wrestling", "weapons", "swords", "armor", "enemies", "fiery darts", "shields", "battles", "fight", "authority", and "strongholds" begin to make sense.

Many believers today live wounded and powerless lives because they don't realize, or take seriously, the reality of this warfare.

Chapter One

The Primary
Theater of Battle

In every major earthly war, there have been significant battles which took place in now-famous theaters/locations that turned the tide of that war to one side. Bull Run, Antietam, and Gettysburg on the Eastern United States Theater during the Civil War; The Battles of Marne and Verdun on the Western Front of Northern France and Belgium during World War I.

Many of us have studied the Battle of Britain, the Battle of Stalingrad, the Invasion of Normandy, and the Battle of the Bulge, all on the Eastern European Theater during World War II - and who can forget Pearl Harbor, Midway, Iwo Jima, Okinawa, Hiroshima and Nagasaki in the Pacific Theater also during World War II. All the great wars were powerfully impacted by these significant theaters of battle.

Satan's primary theater of battle today is our mind. From the very beginning, Satan has had one main strategy in his war against mankind: lies and deception. He doesn't show up with horns and a pitchfork - he shows up with demeaning accusations and deceptive, yet logically sounding suggestions, all of which can sound like the truth. We've all heard them, and we continue to hear the cunning voice of the diabolical "father of lies" almost daily.

We will explore some of these in much greater detail in the chapters ahead.

In the Garden of Eden, Satan didn't attack Eve with force. He attacked her mind. He said, "Did God really say...?" He questioned God's Word. Then, he suggested that God may be holding out on them, questioning His goodness. If you eat the fruit "you will be like God". Thoughts that she pondered long enough to conclude that they could be true. Once she agreed with the enemy's lies, she acted, and sin forever entered the human race.

But even then, God had a plan. He promised that one day, a Savior would come to crush the serpent's (Satan's) head (Genesis 3:15 NIV).

So Satan kept lying. He tried to corrupt the human race that God made "in His image", and to destroy the family line that would eventually lead to Jesus and the fulfillment of God's plan. He used pride, lust, idolatry, and fear to pull people away from God. He stirred up kings, nations, and even God's people to rebel. But God kept His promise - the Savior was born.

The enemy tried again, by convincing the jealous, power-crazed ruler of Judea to slaughter all the young boys in the city of Bethlehem where Jesus was born. In what has since been called, "The Slaughter of the Innocents", King Herod the Great took no chances that this boy being called "King of the Jews" would grow up to replace him. He ordered his soldiers to murder all male children in Bethlehem under the age of two (Matthew 2:16-18). Thankfully, this diabolical plan also failed.

When Jesus began His ministry, Satan questioned Jesus' identity and tried to persuade Him to take shortcuts, forsake God the Father, and worship him instead. While doing so, he also tempted Jesus to take shortcuts: "Turn these stones into bread. Jump off the temple. Bow to me and I'll give you the world." Lies. All of them. Jesus didn't argue—He didn't ponder - He answered immediately with Scripture - the Truth. (See Matthew 4:1-11). As a result, Satan left him alone, temporarily.

And when Satan thought he had finally won by having Jesus crucified, he actually lost everything. The cross was not a defeat of God and His plan—it was God's greatest victory.

Satan's war for the eternal souls of mankind was soundly defeated at the cross of Jesus. Now, all who believe in Jesus' name will be rescued from the kingdom of darkness and transferred into his kingdom of light for all eternity (see Colossians 1:13). Jesus' victory, and gift of eternal life, are available to anyone who believes in Him and receives them (Romans 10:13).

Having been soundly defeated by Jesus, Satan's strategy shifted. He would now focus his troops, and their efforts, on those who embrace Jesus' gift of eternal life and dedicate their lives to following Him and telling others of His kingdom - us.

But how? What strategy, what scheme, what game plan would he use this time? Why not go back to what has worked so well in the past? It worked beautifully in the Garden, and it works effectively today - the battlefield of the mind.

Satan is no dummy. He knows if he can control our mind/thought life, he can control our actions, and subsequently - our life.

As a man thinks in his heart - so is he. Proverbs 23:7

Above all else, guard your heart, or everything you do flows from it.
Proverbs 4:23

Others have realized this truth as well….

"We become what we think about" - Earl Nightingale

"The soul becomes dyed with the color of its thoughts" - Marcus Aurelius

"Change your thoughts and you change your world" - Norman Vincent Peale

"A man is what he thinks about all day long" - Ralph Waldo Emerson

This is exactly why Satan rarely assaults us directly or physically. He is more cunning, more deceptive, more diabolical than that. He operates in the shadows, in the darkness. His is a theater of the soul - the mind, will, and emotions of un-suspecting, uneducated, and vulnerable believers.

His strategy to "kill, steal and destroy" (see John 10:10) is not overt. He knows we would be able to recognize such efforts and stop him. He operates in a the-ater reminiscent of the Vietnam War. He is the enemy who operates covertly, in the darkness, the jungles, the shadows. He hides in thick underbrush, sets booby-traps along our pathways, and has snipers hiding in the thick canopy over-head. We rarely see him coming until we have been wounded.

Satan cannot simply physically kill us, rob us, or destroy us as God's children. His schemes are much more diabolical and sinister. He poisons our thoughts to the point where we literally kill, steal, and destroy ourselves. (Mark 7:20-23). We end up doing his job for him. That is why we must know how he operates and how to never allow him space in our heads.

That is why this book is so important. Not because I have been compelled to write it - but because it could literally save your life, or the life of someone you deeply care about.

> *My people perish for lack of knowledge.*
> Hosea 4:6a

Chapter Two

How Could That Happen?

Let me pause here and tell you a true story about a good friend of mine - let's call him Jeff for the sake of anonymity.

Jeff was a super successful businessman, a devoted husband and father and a mature, deep Christian leader in his church. He taught Bible studies for years, and knew the Scriptures very well. He was a beloved, Christian leader in our community.

As a financially successful man, he was approached regularly by others hoping he would invest in their projects and opportunities. He passed on most of them but found several worthy of his hard-earned money.

All went well until one year, the economy took a turn for the worse, several of those business ventures went south, and he stood to lose substantial amounts of money - so much so that he could have found himself on the verge of financial ruin.

My wife received a phone call from his wife asking if I would get together with Jeff and offer him some encouragement and hope. As a financial/investment advisor myself, she was hopeful I could offer him some support and advice. She said he had become quite despondent and seemed depressed over his situation, and she was worried about him.

I did get together with Jeff over breakfast and encouraged him to "hang in there", and that "God would work things out" for him even though things seemed bleak at the moment. He was in deep debt, but he also had a fantastic income that would be able to pull him out of that debt in a few short years. He appeared encouraged, and I was thankful for the time and opportunity to cheer him up and offer some hope.

A few days later, my wife received another call from Jeff's wife. Through tears, she told her that Jeff's employees had found him in his office. He had committed suicide.

I can't tell you the shockwaves that slammed into our community - and into my own soul. 'How could this happen?' was repeating in my mind like a broken re- cord. "Couldn't he see there was light at the end of his financial tunnel?" "How could someone so versed in the Word and so grounded in the Lord do this?" I was not only saddened - I was upset, confused…and honestly, angry.

About a week after Jeff's funeral, God revealed to me what had really happened. Even though Jeff knew the Bible and was a devoted believer - he had been lis- tening to the wrong voice. He had allowed the arch-enemy of all believers (weak or strong) to lie to him about his financial situation, and convince him that - "he would never recover from his mistakes", that "he was a failure", and "his family would be better off without him", and so much more.

Like Eve in the Garden, Jeff listened to the lies of the enemy, and eventually made an agreement with them - that they were true. That agreement led to acting on the lies, and the result was catastrophic. We will discuss this in much greater detail in the book, but for now, suffice it to say that what God showed me through that traumatic event continues to drive me today to do what I can to alert and embolden my brothers and sisters in Christ to - WAKE UP!

Don't fall for the schemes, the deceptions, the lies our enemy whispers to us ev- ery day. Learn to fight! Learn to live victoriously!

The only power the enemy has over you is the power you give him! Satan didn't kill Jeff.….he convinced Jeff to do it for him.

Lisa's story is sadly similar to Jeff's but with a much different outcome. She was a popular, happy, healthy high schooler who had everything going for her. A

Christian young lady with a good family, good friends, good looks, good future - what could go wrong?

Over the first semester of her senior year, students, teachers, and parents alike began noticing big changes in Lisa. She was losing weight - too much weight - and she began withdrawing from family and friends. Her grades dropped, and her happy-go-lucky demeanor changed. When asked if she was okay, she would answer everyone, "Yes, I'm fine". No one wanted to pry, but suspected maybe she was ill and just didn't want to talk about it.

Lisa's parents began to worry and finally convinced her to talk to some close Christian friends of theirs. All went predictably fine during the early, surface-level part of their discussion, but when asked to explain why she was losing so much weight, she exposed the darkness that had been tormenting her for months.

She calmly replied, "When I look at myself in the mirror, a voice tells me 'I'm fat, and ugly, and need to lose weight'. Whenever she saw herself in a mirror, or a reflection in a window, etc., she had those self-deprecating, self-destructive thoughts - and interpreted them as her own thoughts…and true.

She heard them so often, she came to believe what they "said" was the truth. Then, when she agreed with the thoughts, they became her truth - "I am" those things.

Then, as Proverbs 23 says - she became fat and ugly in her own mind - and began acting upon those thoughts.

Truth is, she was anything but fat or ugly. She was very attractive and not overweight in the least. In her mind, however, she sincerely believed she was. She had taken the bait, believed the lie - just like Eve, just like Jeff - and was heading towards a similarly destructive end.

The enemy was stealing - her health, her vitality, her joy, her future, her life. He had set her on a self-destructive course that would not only steal from her - but ultimately get her to destroy herself.

Thankfully, God through parents, friends, counselors, and many prayers, opened her eyes to the deception she had believed. She renounced it and with God's help, restored her health and her future.

Chapter Three

Think About It

So, how did Satan gain access to Jeff and Lisa's thought life, and how does he gain access to ours?

Thoughts bombard our mind every minute of every day.

A 2020 peer-reviewed neuroscience study that used brain imaging to track "thought transitions" in real time determined that the average human has somewhere around 6,000 thoughts per day. (Queen's University, Kingston, Ontario - published by Nature Magazine). While not definitive, the conclusion is clear - we have thousands of thoughts running through our minds every single day of our lives.

According to the Bible, these thoughts emanate from:

1. God (directly, and through His Word and prayer).

2. Ourselves (greatly influenced by our flesh, our culture, our past/present hurts, as well as past/present sin patterns and habits).

3. Satan/demons (directly planting thoughts in our mind and indirectly through influencing prevailing worldview, political, educational, and cultural propaganda, media of all kinds, and ungodly peers/friends).

A non-Christian cannot hear the voice of God since the Bible says he/she is "dead" (spiritually), and God's thoughts must be spiritually discerned. (See 1 Corinthians 2:14). The non-believer also has no defense against the regular bombardment of evil, destructive, negative thoughts being launched from the "father of lies".

Christians, on the other hand, have the Spirit of God now living inside them, in their innermost being, their spirit. They have the capacity to not only hear the voice of God and to discern wisdom and understanding through the Bible, but also to commune with God personally every day.

Years ago a good friend in our small group meeting hit the nail on the head. During our discussion regarding these things, he quietly said, "We just need to think about what we think about". Everyone stopped. That's it. That's the bottom line.

Our thoughts are influenced greatly by multiple sources: the Word of God, the sermons we hear, the music we listen to, the media we consume, the culture, our friends and family, Satan's whispers (Matthew16:23) and many others. We can't just sit back and allow every thought, from every source, colored by multiple worldly sources, to just run through our minds unfettered, 24/7.

As believers, we must learn the critical discipline of taking our thoughts captive, and making them obedient (comply with, subordinate to) Christ's truth.

>   …"*we take captive every thought to make it obedient to Christ.*"
>   2 Corinthians 10:5b NIV

He (Jesus) went on: "What comes out of a person is what defiles them. For it is from within, out of a person's heart, that evil thoughts come—sexual immorality, theft, murder, adultery, greed, malice, deceit, lewdness, envy, slander, arrogance and folly. All these evils come from inside and defile a person."

Mark 7:20-23 NIV

Why is this so important?

We need to be ever-vigilant in guarding the gateways to our mind, the doorways to our thoughts and actions. King Solomon, reportedly the wisest, most respected man of his time - gave us the ultimate "bottom line" message regarding the importance of keeping watch over our thought life.

> *"Guard your heart (mind) above all else, for it*
> *determines the course of your life."*
> Proverbs 4:23 NLT

Satan knows if he can win the battle for control of your mind/thoughts, he can control your actions, and subsequently the course of your life. He was successful in doing so with my friend Jeff, and was dangerously close with Lisa as well.

We need to spend some time talking about how the enemy gains access to our mind, and how to keep him from it.

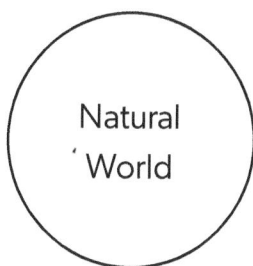

We all live in the natural world. This is the world of our senses; what we can see, hear, touch, taste, and smell. The world of science, and what we can measure, yet a world of art, of music, and beauty. We are told not to believe anything we can't define, measure, or experience through these means. Most of us live our lives focused on what is right in front of us - work, school, friends, family, church, responsibilities, bills, hobbies, and daily routines.

But, God's Word tells us there is another dimension to life; another world, one that is as real, and in fact, more permanent than the one we see all around us. Philippians 3:20 reminds us that "Our citizenship is in heaven". From cover to cover, the Bible tells us of God, Satan, heaven, hell, angels, demons, eternity, and kingdoms - a world of the supernatural. An unseen realm, but like the wind, is tangibly experienced still.

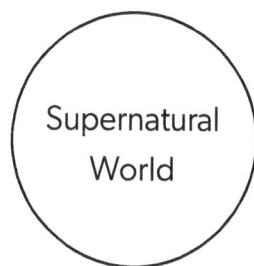

As followers of Jesus, we must remember that we live in both the natural and the supernatural worlds. C.S. Lewis wrote in The Abolition of Man, "we are amphibians, so to speak - creatures called to live both in the clay of Earth and in the fire of Heaven". Understanding this truth changes everything about how we see our purpose, our battles, and our future.

Satan and his demons are supernatural beings, yet they were expelled from heaven down to earth - our natural world. They inhabit the natural world as supernatural, unseen beings. The middle circle is the realm where they interact with us in Our World.

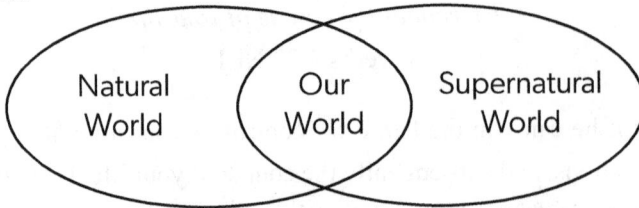

Natural World   Our World   Supernatural World

All of us are born into the natural world, but are also supernatural beings. (See Genesis 2:7), possessing a spirit, soul, and body (1 Thessalonians 5:23). As believers, Satan knows he cannot directly infiltrate or influence our spirit. And, while he can assault and torment us in the natural world (see Luke 13:10-13 and Acts 19:13-16), his primary approach is to patiently, deliberately, patrol the world of our mind (soul) looking for open doors of opportunity.

Think of these doors as access points that allow the enemy the opportunity to gain entrance into an area of our life. Before we become believers, every door to our heart, mind, and soul was open. Like the swinging door in an old-time Western movie, the enemy had free rein to come and go, and to set up shop (establish strongholds, even bondage), in areas of our life.

You may have become a Christian at a young age and have very few such areas in your soul, or you may discover a great many such fortresses have been established in your life if you became a believer much later. We will address and deal with those a little later. The heart of this book is designed to help you identify any territory you may have given the enemy before coming to Christ, take back what the enemy has stolen, and demolish any stronghold he may have been allowed to erect in the past. We will also discuss how to shut any open doors and avoid allowing the enemy any access in the future.

A word of caution - this book will ask you to take action, not just read the words and put it on the shelf with the rest of your Christian collection. Warfare is battle, and we're about to engage. If you've had enough - if you're tired of failing, losing battles with temptation, or feeling powerless to change past propensities and habits - let's go on the offensive ...

Chapter Four

Open Doors

So, how does Satan gain access to our thought life?

In the Book of Job (Chapter 1), God asks Satan, "From where have you come?" Satan replies, "From going to and fro on the earth, and from walking up and down on it".

Peter reminds believers in 1 Peter 5:8 - *"Be sober-minded; be watchful. Your adversary the devil prowls around like a roaring lion, seeking someone to devour"*.

Remember, Satan and one third of the angels were booted out of heaven because of their rebellion against God - and where did they go? They we "cast down" to earth - this same physical, natural world we call our planet, our world, our home. So, in that intersection of the natural and supernatural worlds - the "circle" we labeled "Our World" a few pages back - the enemy and his armies prowl, walk to and fro, relentlessly, without rest - looking for "someone to devour". You need to know, the Greek and Jewish perspective of "devour" literally means, "to engulf", "to consume", and is used to convey total destruction or consumption - "absolute ruin".

Our enemy is ot kidding around. Our war is not an athletic contest where one team wins and another loses and everyone goes home and enjoys life until the next game. We are up against an enemy force hell-bent on our complete and total physical, mental, and emotional destruction. That is why we must be "sober-minded", deliberate, serious, equally committed to keeping the enemy from destroying our lives and the lives of those we love.

While there are certainly Biblical examples of demons tormenting someone's physical body - see Matthew 9:32-33, Matthew 12:22, Matthew 17:14-18, Mark 9:25, Luke 13:11, Luke 9:37-42 - the primary battleground for Satan's destructive activity is our mind. If he can control our thoughts, he can control our actions. If he can control our actions, he can control our life, and our destiny.

Knock Knock

As the enemy prowls around the perimeter of our life, he is constantly looking to gain entrance via our thought life. Think of an ancient city or castle with a high wall around it. Instead of one or maybe two entry gates to that fortified city - in our case, there are many doors, many entrance points allowing or preventing access.

As an unbeliever, every door to our mind/thinking is open. Due to the sin of Adam, we enter "Our World" with every door wide open to whatever comes knocking.

Our lives are unguarded and completely open to Satan's influence and activity.

Genesis 6:5 - *The Lord saw how great the wickedness of the human race had become on the earth, and that every inclination of the thoughts of the human heart was only evil all the time.*

Ephesians 2:1-3 - *As for you, you were dead in your transgressions and sins, in which you used to live when you followed the ways of this world and of the ruler of the kingdom of the air, the spirit who is now at work in those who are disobedient. All of us also lived among them at one time, gratifying the cravings of our flesh and following its desires and thoughts. Like the rest, we were by nature deserving of wrath.*

The moment we accept Christ as our Lord and Savior, we not only receive the amazing gift of eternal life, but we are ushered into a new kingdom. We are transported from our original spiritual domain, the "kingdom of darkness" ruled by Satan himself, to our new, spiritual dwelling place - the kingdom of God.

Colossians 1:13-14 - *For he (God) has rescued us from the dominion of darkness and brought us into the kingdom of the Son he loves, in whom we have redemption, the forgiveness of sins.*

Trouble is - we are literally now residents of the spiritual kingdom of our Father, God, but we still live physically in the earthly kingdom of darkness. Thankfully, in this new domain, we are given the gift of the Holy Spirit of God to both indwell us and become the Watchman on the "wall" around our mind/thoughts.

Proverbs 18:2 - *The Lord is my rock, my fortress and my deliverer 'my God is my rock, in whom I take refuge.*

Proverbs 18:10 - *The name of the Lord is a fortified tower; the righteous run to it and are safe.*

The Spirit of God now lives inside us and becomes the "tower guard" over our mind…if we allow Him. Our minds are, however, still ultimately under our authority. We control what we allow inside, and what we keep out. That's why we are encouraged to "guard our heart", to "be alert", etc. It is not God's responsibility to do this. Even though we live in a fortress of protection, we are still given the keys that open or close the doors to the "outside" world. We can lock them or choose to leave them open. Many believers struggle with ongoing sin and torment from the enemy simply because they have kept the doors open to the outside world of darkness. Many more discover an open door, close it, and then allow Satan to open a different one…the cycle repeats.

We also need to realize two significant things:

1. Before our salvation, we unknowingly allowed the enemy to plant thoughts, opinions, reasonings, and what we came to think of as "truths" in our minds. Some of us have decades of such earthly, ungodly, unscriptural, hurtful, evil thoughts, ideas and presumptions that have built up high walls, called strongholds, in our thinking. Becoming a Christian doesn't automatically demolish such walls nor change our thinking patterns. Those years of Satan-influenced thoughts, deceptions, lies, etc. need to be dealt with - and we will do so later in the book.

2. After salvation, we need to take responsibility for the "guarding of our heart". We, along with help from the Holy Spirit, must make conscious

choices daily, and even throughout the day, to "take our thoughts captive". It is incumbent on us (not God, not the church) to "put on the whole armor of God" (Ephesians 6), to "set our minds on things above" (Colossians 3), to "be transformed by the renewing of our mind" (Romans 12), to "walk in the Spirit" (Galatians 5), and to "be alert" (1 Peter 5:8) to the schemes and tactic of the devil. If we are slack in doing these things, or fail altogether, we choose to leave old doors open, or take our keys and open other doors. In doing so, we set ourselves up for disaster.

We will explore both of these in greater detail, but for now, let's go back to "open doors".

Every moment of every day, Satan and his minions prowl around the "walls" of our mind/heart, checking to see if there are any "doors" left open or if there might be even a crack, a small opening, in which to gain a foothold for entry. If they find an open door, or if they can convince you to "answer" the door they are knocking on and open it yourself, they will gladly come in and begin establishing a foothold. If not dealt with, that foothold will become a stronghold and much more difficult to demolish. If that stronghold is not destroyed (see 2 Corinthians 10:3-5), it will grow and become increasingly stronger to the point of spiritual, emotional, and even physical bondage.

The easiest believer for Satan to "devour" is the one who has no supernatural security system. It is up to us to set up and maintain such a system. This is why Solomon said "guarding our heart" was the activity believers should focus on "above all else".

A longtime, Christian brother and friend worked long hours as a medical professional. He was on his feet all day and most often bent over his patients performing delicate procedures. Over time, he developed very painful back problems that threatened to shorten, or even end, his career. As a medical professional, he also had access to pharmaceuticals. He began hearing the "voice" suggesting (tempting, wooing) that he needed to ease his pain in order to continue working and supporting his family. At first, the "thought" seemed very rational - a very logical solution.

An accompanying "thought" assured him that as a Christian, and a trained medical professional, he would be well able to control his use of a pain-killing med.

And, so he did…until the original dose wasn't numbing the pain all day. "Just a little more" seemed appropriate since he was "handling it" just fine at work. Well, you probably know the rest of the story - but he eventually became addicted, and nearly lost his livelihood altogether. Rehab and much prayer kept him from being "devoured".

The enemy's intention is always to "kill, steal, and destroy." (John 10:10) He is never content with anything less than total destruction. Don't be fooled - he is pure evil and is relentless. His "forces of darkness" patiently listen to your words, observe your life, and determine where you have a weakness, a vulnerability, a door left cracked open by things like - a childhood hurt or loss; a demeaning, hurtful comment years ago; an emotionally abusive parent, spouse, coach, or boss, etc. - and he knocks on that door.

We all have them; those wounds from our past. Some long, long ago - some more recent. We all deal with them in different ways, but they are still there, still painful to the touch. In the following Chapter, we will begin to unpack these wounds and what to do about them.

Chapter Five

Agreements

So, how does Satan gain access to our thought life? Here is a word you need to know, add to your Christian vocabulary, and be conscious of at all times... AGREEMENT.

Let's start at the beginning.

Now the serpent was more crafty than any of the wild animals the Lord God had made. He said to the woman, "Did God really say, 'You must not eat from any tree in the garden'?" The woman said to the serpent, "We may eat fruit from the trees in the garden, but God did say, 'You must not eat fruit from the tree that is in the middle of the garden, and you must not touch it, or you will die.'"

"You will not certainly die," the serpent said to the woman. "For God knows that when you eat from it your eyes will be opened, and you will be like God, knowing good and evil." When the woman saw that the fruit of the tree was good for food and pleasing to the eye, and also desirable for gaining wisdom, she took some and ate it. She also gave some to her husband, who was with her, and he ate it. Genesis 3:1-6

Satan cast doubt on God's words and what she actually heard; then he lied about God's word and planted doubt in Eve's mind (and obviously Adam's too since he was there with her). The key phrase is verse 6 - "when the woman saw (surely she had seen the fruit during this discussion), but this time she saw "that it was:

a) "good for food", b) "pleasing to the eye", and c) "desirable for gaining wisdom"... she then took it and ate.

Did you catch that? Satan didn't assault her or threaten her or scare her. He carefully, deceptively got her to doubt what God had said, then the reason God said it. She went from innocent and sincere obedience to questioning God's intentions and goodness - all with just some cleverly orchestrated thoughts planted in her innocent mind.

Verse 6, however, is where the damage was done. She could have seen that the fruit looked good and might certainly taste delicious - and could have simply stopped there - but see what happened next.

In order for her to come to the conclusion that the fruit was also *desirable for gaining wisdom,* she made a decision - an AGREEMENT, with Satan's lies - and that is what compelled her to take a bite. She agreed with what Satan said and decided she wanted what he was suggesting. Her agreement led to her action.

Something similar, but much less devastating to the human race, occurred in the life of King David.

In the spring, at the time when kings go off to war, David sent Joab out with the king's men and the whole Israelite army. They destroyed the Ammonites and besieged Rabbah. But David remained in Jerusalem.

One evening, David got up from his bed and walked around on the roof of the palace. From the roof, he saw a woman bathing. The woman was very beautiful, and David sent someone to find out about her. The man said, "She is Bathsheba, the daughter of Eliam and the wife of Uriah the Hittite." Then David sent messengers to get her. She came to him, and he slept with her. 2 Samuel 11:1-4

Kings always went off to war with their troops. Was David ill, or have some other legitimate reason for staying behind in Jerusalem? Did he stay home because he had seen this same beautiful woman bathing at night from his rooftop before, and had hatched a scheme to stay behind for more clandestine reasons? We don't know for sure.

Let's go with this "sighting" being his first. We will give him the benefit of the doubt. So, we assume the king can't sleep and gets up to walk around and get

28

some fresh air. He goes out on the rooftop patio and happens to see a gorgeous woman bathing in the night. Here is David's moment of truth - his "Eve" moment.

Innocent or not - he was hearing the voice of the same Tempter that was successful in making Eve and Adam fall.

Obviously, he observed that the woman was naked and beautiful - that's a no-brainer". But, the enemy wasn't content with simply causing this great King to lust after another man's wife - oh no - he wants destruction remember? He begins to plant thoughts (suggestions) that sound like "What would it be like to…?" "You are the king and you can have her if you want". "I wonder if she is married, and if she is, her husband is probably out in the war." Regardless, he was being bombarded with thoughts of lust, adultery, and more.

Like all of us faced with sinful thoughts - he had a decision to make: Reject the suggestions/lies to indulge himself, or flee - turn away and leave the temptation behind.

What does David do? Same thing Eve did - he pondered, he considered, he reasoned, he justified, he rationalized - and then he made an AGREEMENT with the lies…and acted. Again, with devastating consequences.

Do you see how that works? Satan doesn't "make" you do anything. He plants lies. He knocks on a door of vulnerability in your mind and tries to get you to open it by making an agreement with him. When you agree with a lie, you open a door and invite him in, and grant him permission to start setting up shop - establishing a foothold in that area of your life - a foothold that becomes a stronghold, brick by brick, until it is high and strong and hard to bring down.

Ephesians 4:27 speaks of giving the devil a "foothold" in our life by harboring anger and unforgiveness. The Greek definition of "foothold" is "topos" or "territory". We can open a door into our soul and give our mortal enemy "territory", or "space", to begin building a fortress - a "stronghold" there.

Remember Jesus' words: He went on: "What comes out of a person is what defiles them. For it is from within, out of a person's heart, that evil thoughts come— sexual immorality, theft, murder, adultery, greed, malice, deceit, lewdness, envy, slander, arrogance and folly. All these evils come from inside and defile a person." Mark 7:20-23 NIV

All sin begins small. A single thought or action can lead to a lifetime of addiction to alcohol, drugs, smoking, gambling, pornography, etc. No one addicted to these things set out to become an addict, living their life in turmoil, pain and sorrow.

If an escaped murderer/rapist came to your door and knocked, would you gladly open the door and welcome him inside to meet your wife and children? Christians everywhere are doing this very thing in the spiritual realm regularly - and are clueless as to why their marriages and families are being assaulted and destroyed.

Satan and his army cannot kick in our "doors". They roam around our lives observing, listening, watching, and knocking - to find any door left open from the past, or any "door" that they feel you might open with the right lie or deception.

God spoke to Adam's son, Cain, and warned him that, "sin is crouching at your door" in Genesis 4:7. This is a great word picture of sin (Satan/demons/evil) crouching in a doorway where they detect weakness and vulnerability - waiting for you to crack it open, even slightly, giving them opportunity to rush inside.

We all have doors - many doors. All along the perimeter of our heart/mind. We have doors that have been formed in years past, others we have opened recently, and still more he will no doubt try to get us to open in the future. We must take the time to deal with the old and the recent and to set up a security system to guard the new ones.

Let's unpack that last thought...

Chapter Six

The Old Doors

Middle school is weird. Middle school is hard.

Many of my old agreements started in middle school - (we old-timers called it Junior High School).

You see, when I was in elementary school - I was somebody. I was always picked first when we chose sides to play kickball, dodgeball, football, you name it - I was "the one" everyone wanted on their team. I could out-run, out-throw, out-kick every other kid in school. Life was goooood.

Then came - junior high school.

Without any warning, I was thrown in with boys with facial hair, body hair - boys several inches taller than me....and with muscles. I was doomed. I went from being "king of the hill" to not being able to even get on the hill. Physical Education (P.E.) class was a daily exercise in humiliation. I was a rag doll to be tossed around in wrestling class, and went home dirty and sweaty after school because I was too embarrassed to take showers (yes, we did that back then too) with these grown men they called peers.

I was physically much smaller and thus, weaker than most of the guys trying out for sports. In addition, I came from a divorced home, and my sweet mother had to work to support my brother and me. I had to walk to and from school carrying my football gear in a pillow case - which only added to my embarrassment. We didn't have much money, so my clothes weren't the "cool" fashions of the day. So - I didn't fit in with the "cool kids" from the higher-class neighborhoods. It is sad how much peer pressure shapes our early thinking about ourselves, and about life.

It was there that my earliest agreements were formed. Thoughts like, "I'm not as good as....", or "I'm not as cool as....." haunted me nearly every day.

Coaches' demeaning words reinforced thoughts of "I'm not good enough" or "I will never be able to......". My seventh grade year (first year in junior high) was the year of "failure". The enemy seized every opportunity to whisper thoughts of failure, insecurity, self-doubt, and hopelessness. He whispered things "you are a woos, a loser, a wimp", "you don't have what it takes", "you will never be good enough"....so often that it didn't take long for me to make agreements with every one of the lies - and the "**you** don't....." became "**I** don't". I agreed, and then the lies became my reality.

Do you see how that happens? Words spoken over us, or to us - family and financial circumstances - athletics - peers - social media - the enemy uses any and every opportunity and avenue, to speak lies and deceptions to us, hoping we will make agreements in our mind. When we do, he convinces us that we "are" those lies and deceptions. Whether we are young or old, he never stops trying. His goal is to get you and me to embrace (agree with) his lies, knowing that we will become what we think we are.

Have you ever had thoughts that whisper...

- You're not good enough. You can't do anything right. You're just a loser.

- You're just like your father/mother. You were just born that way.

- You don't fit in. No one loves you. You're not wanted.

- You're on your own. No one cares. God doesn't really love you.

- You'll never change. You're just a screw-up.

Have you possibly made agreements with any of them?

We have ALL been exposed. Words, voices, thoughts from our past - spoken about us, spoken to us, spoken over us - innocently or on purpose - and they matter. They hurt. They wounded something deep in our soul. Our enemy whispered them so often that we started to believe them, and along with that belief (agreement) came the pronoun shift from "You" to "I". Instead of the demeaning lie that "you aren't good enough", we started believing "I am not good enough". That agreement began shaping who we said we were, and that belief shaped who we became.

I heard the voice of failure so often, I subconsciously lived with a fear, and yet an expectation, that I would fail at most things I attempted. As a newlywed trying to support my family on commissioned insurance sales, I struggled. I was once again failing. When a prospect said "no" or "not now," - I heard it again…. I had failed.

I can vividly remember years later, while all the men in our church small group were visiting in our host's kitchen - it seemed all the other guys were buying vacation homes, new cars, building new homes, etc. - and once again the thoughts surfaced, "you'll never be successful like these guys", "you're family deserves more than you can provide", "you're a failure", "you aren't a good husband, father, provider". They came flooding in, and with each thought I could feel the emotions of envy, jealousy, and shame sweep over me.

That was years after my boyhood struggles, and yet, they were still there, still loud, still powerful - still hurtful.

Unless we take the time to deal with the agreements of our past and close those doors, we will continue to live as walking wounded, not whole, not free - susceptible to attack at any time.

There is no time like the present, so let me encourage you to stop right here for a minute. Put the book down, and think. Grab a pen and paper and ask God to show you any agreements you may have made in your past with the lies of the enemy. Some places to begin should include agreements you may have made about:

- Yourself - your appearance, your intelligence, your performance (school, sports, etc.), your self-esteem, your family, social or financial status, your friendships, your family relationships, etc. Thoughts like, "I always", or

"I will never, or I can't". What do you truly think about yourself? How do you compare to others? What do you believe others think/feel about you?

- God - unanswered prayer; why He allowed suffering; has He really forgiven your sins; feeling that He didn't come through when you needed Him, questioning His love for you; feeling He's disappointed or displeased with you, etc.

- Family & Friends - did my father and mother love me; unkind, cruel or hurtful words spoken over me; my status in my peer group; how I compared with my sibling(s); not feeling included or part of the "in" crowd; feelings of being treated unfairly; jealousy; envy - feeling inferior or "lesser than", etc.

- What else does God bring to mind?

*For the **accuser** of our brothers and sisters, who accuses them before our God day and night, has been hurled down.* Rev. 12:10

Make no mistake - no agreement with demonic accusations, lies, or deceptions is acceptable. We must all take the time to get with God and deal with every single one He reveals to us. We can not afford to leave one wall erected or one door open.

His lies can lead to our demise, as we have seen, but more often they lead to a life marked by anxiety, fear, depression, loneliness, insecurity, shame, addiction, and more. This is not the abundant life promised by Jesus in John 10:10.

Satan is thrilled to keep believers in such a constant state of busyness, distraction, and emotional torment that they never discover and address their crippling agreements with his lies and accusations, which renders them joyless and fruitless in their Christian life. Take whatever time necessary to identify them. We will discuss what to do with them a bit later. This is a critical step to living in freedom and joy.

God's Voice	Satan's Voice
• Stills you	• Rushes you
• Leads you	• Pushes you
• Reassures you	• Frightens you
• Enlightens you	• Confuses you
• Encourages you	• Discourages you
• Comforts you	• Worries you
• Calms you	• Obsesses you
• Convicts you	• Condemns you

Chapter Seven

Existing &
Future Doors

The exercise in the previous chapter is crucial if we expect to live in freedom and enjoy the abundance of the life He died to give us. As unbelievers, we ALL allowed lies and accusations, along with hurtful, cruel, demeaning, and deceitful thoughts and words, free rein in our minds. We also lived a life marked by sinful thoughts and actions, moral compromise, and disobedience to God and His Word. (see Ephesians 2:3). Whether spoken by others or spoken to ourselves, we made agreements with our mortal enemy and gave him territory in our mind/heart. He does not automatically give up that territory when we become Christians.

We must take the exercise in Chapter 6 seriously. That territory must be regained if we are to live the abundant life as children of the King. Don't move on until you have identified the primary strongholds that were erected in your past. Remember - strongholds have been defined as:

"any area in your life where you find it easier to think or do what
Satan says, than what God says"

"a faulty belief system rooted in Satan's deceptions and lies that
keeps you in emotional bondage" - or -

"spiritual castles in the mind where the devil controls lives
through wrong belief systems and lies".

[And don't forget, the biggest deception of all is that we don't have any faulty beliefs or agreements from our past to deal with. You've probably already heard that whispered while reading this.]

There is an entire chapter ahead discussing strongholds, so we will unpack that much more thoroughly.

As you begin to identify strongholds from the past, God will begin revealing current thoughts, words, and actions that have left "doors" open for the enemy. These also need to be closed as soon as possible. Any open door is an entry point, and an invitation for Satan's disruptive and destructive work in your life.

After accepting Christ, it is the believer's responsibility to set up a 24/7/365 security system. Much like the commercial door cameras at my home, this new spiritual security system notifies you when "someone" is on your premises, lurking, knocking, crouching. Once identified, it is our responsibility, again, to decide if the visiting knock (thought) is from God or from Satan.

Important to note - the responsibility to 'guard our heart' rests on us. It is not automatically provided at our salvation. What IS provided is the new indwelling of God's Holy Spirit. In a manner of speaking, the Spirit becomes our God-consciousness, our early-warning system against enemy attacks. Make no mistake though, the Bible is crystal clear that it is not God's responsibility to "guard our heart", to "keep alert", "be watchful" - but ours.

The Spirit:

- convicts us of sin

- bears witness of Christ (reminds us of all he has done for us)

- brings God's Word to our remembrance

- teaches us God's Word and its application

- bears fruit in our lives if we yield to Him

- alerts us to danger and deception

It is our responsibility to be attentive to His voice. We choose every day whether to "walk in the Spirit" or "walk in the flesh"; whether to "set our mind" on the "things of the flesh or the things of the Spirit". These are choices we make that ensure our alarm system is armed, and that we are "alert" to the danger.

Those who live according to the flesh have their minds set on what the flesh desires; but those who live in accordance with the Spirit have their minds set on what the Spirit desires. Romans 8:5

So I say, walk by the Spirit, and you will not gratify the desires of the flesh. For the flesh desires what is contrary to the Spirit, and the Spirit what is contrary to the flesh. They are in conflict with each other, so that you are not to do whatever you want. Galatians 5:17

Set your minds on things above, not on earthly things. Colossians 3:2

Finally, brothers and sisters, whatever is true, whatever is noble, whatever is right, whatever is pure, whatever is lovely, whatever is admirable—if anything is excellent or praiseworthy—think about such things. Philippians 4:8

It is pretty obvious. If we want to be led by the Spirit, We have to DO things. Again, it is our responsibility to: "set our minds", "walk by the Spirit", and "think on these things". That means - we must live deliberately. We have to develop the daily discipline of doing what God says to do. By doing so - we develop a more sophisticated security system - we learn how to "guard our heart/mind", and live each day "on alert, on guard" (1 Peter 5:8).

Bottom line is this - we need to take the time to get alone with God and uncover the open doors from our past (write them down as He reveals them, so we can deal with them). Next, we need to get busy developing a daily strategy for reading and meditating in God's Word, and praying for the Spirit to lead and guide us into all truth. A quick devotional reading, or 5-minute "quiet time", is woefully inadequate to accomplish what we need to accomplish.

Do we really want to walk in freedom or not?

Anything significant in my life that I ever wished to accomplish - took work - it required discipline to achieve.

- playing baseball, football, tennis, swimming, etc.

- learning to play the guitar, water ski, snow ski, golf

- making good enough grades in school to get accepted to college

- learning to excel in a new career

- getting in shape, eating properly, staying in shape

- becoming a good husband and father

Becoming proficient in anything in life requires discipline and sacrifice. Our spiritual life is no exception. The Bible makes this point very clear in Galatians 6:7, that we "will reap what we sow".

If we become aware of Satan's schemes, his strategy for erecting strongholds in our mind, as well as our own open doors allowing him access and permission to torment us - but do nothing about them - we shouldn't expect anything to change for the better in our lives.

If you know these things, happy are you if you do them.
John 13:17

Chapter Eight

Cleaning Your Mental House

It has been said that if you want to rid a home of rats, you need to get rid of their food. In order to rid your thought life of the rats of the past, you have to throw out their food and run them out of town. You began doing that in the last chapter.

Simultaneously, you started working on setting up a more efficient, powerful security system to guard against future incursions of "rats".

Hopefully, you now have a list of "rats" - lies, deceptions, wounds, etc. - from your past that you have carried all your life. One of mine was - inadequacy ("you don't have what it takes"), which is typically accompanied by Satan's accusation that "you are a failure". I was aware that I had feelings of inadequacy from time to time in teenage sports, peer pressure, social status, etc., but I assumed these would just go away as I got older. Honestly, I didn't think about those thoughts/ feelings much at all - they just popped up on occasion.

As a Christian adult, however, I began paying more attention to those thoughts. I found myself comparing myself to other worship leaders and men in my church. Thoughts like, "you're not as spiritual as he is", or "you don't know how to pray like he does" often spoke to me, along with the old faithful, "you don't measure up as a husband and father", "you're not as successful as he is", and, "your family will never have what theirs has".

Do you see how that works? The enemy (the accuser) relentlessly looks for any opportunity to poke an old wound, a bruise from the past that is still tender. Given an opening, he pokes that wounded spot in your soul to see if he can once again get you to make an agreement with it. Old wounds are doors that have remained cracked open, and are more susceptible to being easily opened again. If they are not closed and locked, chances are we will most likely reopen them.

One of the many things we all have in common is - We have all heard the cunning, deceiving voice of our arch-enemy, Satan.

Many of us very early in our lives, and others much later - but none of us is exempt. He has been lying, deceiving, and accusing mankind since the very first humans were created, and he continues his offensive against you and me.

In our life, many of these lies were spoken by other people, like parents, siblings, teachers, coaches, friends, bosses, colleagues, and even strangers. Take a couple of minutes, set the book aside, and think about those people in your life, and see if you recall anything they may have ever spoken to you, or about you, that sounded like:

  You're just stupid/dumb/slow.
  Why can't you be like your brother/sister?
  You don't belong here. You don't fit in.
  You weren't invited.
  No one wants to be your friend.
  You're just like your father/mother.
  You'll never change.
  You always screw things up.
  You'll always be …
  You're not good enough.
  You don't have what it takes.
  You'll never amount to anything.
  You're too slow/fat/weak/ugly.

The list is almost endless. If not one of the above, think about the people in your life - past and present - who may have spoken such things over you - and write at least one of them down - right here - in the book. I'll help you out by writing in a couple of the many I have dealt with personally:

- You'll never be good enough.

- You'll never be part of the "in" crowd. You don't belong.

- You're a failure and will never be successful.

See how easy that was? Now it's your turn…

_____

_____

_____

Most of the time, the demeaning, negative thoughts and accusations come from within (via Satan's voice) more than from others. We interpret someone's actions or reactions, their words, their tone, the look on their face, and even their body language - and create our own mental narrative of what we assume they must be thinking or feeling about us. Satan seizes the opportunity to begin spewing his accusations, deceptions, and lies into your mind for us to contemplate.

Let's take one of my "rats" and discover how God led me to silence it …. "you're not good enough", "you're a failure", "you don't have what it takes". This rat speaks the same accusation in multiple ways, but the message is still the same.

So step #1 is to Identify the Lie. I had to acknowledge that I had made an agreement with this lie, and had done so multiple times. I had allowed the enemy "territory" in my mind, and he had built a stronghold there over time that was substantial. He used the pronoun "you", but I had changed it to "I" by making those repeated agreements. I had come to believe the "truth" was, that I really was a failure, inadequate, lesser than. It had subtly become part of my identity.

Step #2 is to Identify God's Truth. Over time, and through a study of "Who I am in Christ", and of God's deep and personal love for me, I began to realize that my true identity was not a result of what I thought about myself, or what I perceived others thought about me, but what God thought about me. **See Appendix A**

When Satan challenged Jesus' identity in the wilderness (see Matthew 4:1-11), Jesus didn't receive it or even give his lies the time of day - he immediately spoke God's Word. He spoke the truth! Satan tried three times to get Jesus to pause and consider his lies, but each time Jesus refused and immediately rebuffed him with the Truth. This is what the Bible means when it tells us - *"We destroy arguments and every lofty opinion raised against the knowledge of God, and take every thought captive to obey Christ"* in 2 Corinthians 10:5.

The crucial point to know here is - you can't refute Satan's lies with God's truth if you don't know God's truth. Jesus knew who he was and was not going to give Satan's accusations a second's thought.

I used to think that reading my Bible was an exercise required to be a good Christian, and I seemed to always struggle to "find the time" to fit a quick read into my busy life. After realizing that I live in a literal war zone, it became quite clear that reading God's Word, and knowing what it said, were crucial, not only to my Christian maturity, but also to walking in freedom and victory over my mortal enemy. That is why we are told the Word of God is our primary offensive weapon against Satan's attacks in Ephesians 6:17. I finally learned that knowing God's Word isn't optional, or simply a Christian discipline - I can't wield that powerful Sword if I don't know what it says, and learn how to use it in battle.

Back to my rat.

God led me on a study of who I am in God's eyes, and not simply in my own, or in the eyes of others.

It was there that I discovered:

- I am so deeply loved by God that Jesus suffered and died a gruesome death for me - Romans 5:8, Galatians 2:20, John 15:13, 1 John 3:16

- I am adopted into God's family and part of His Kingdom - 1 John 3:1

- He chose me before I was born - Psalm 139:13-14, Matthew 10:30-31

- He has great plans for me - Ephesians 2:10, Jeremiah 29:11

- I am a joint heir with Christ of His kingdom - Romans 8:17

- God knows me personally and considers me His son - Galatians 4:6

These are but a sampling of the many references in Scripture that remind me of my true identity. I am not "lesser than" - I am a beloved child of the King of

Kings and a joint heir with Jesus of His eternal kingdom. I am not "a failure" - I am chosen by God, Who has great plans for me that He has promised to bring about in my life. I am not "inadequate", but quite the opposite is true - "*I can do all things through Christ who strengthens me*" (Philippians 4:13) - and I am "*more than a conqueror through Him*" (Romans 8:37).

Knowing what God says about me not only revealed to me my true identity as a child of God, but it equipped me with the sword of Truth that I can wield whenever Satan knocks on that particular door in my thoughts. I can immediately rebuff his lies with the truth of God's Word. This is what is meant by "taking thoughts captive to obey Christ" (and His Word). Knowing and professing God's Truth not only tears down existing strongholds, but it keeps new ones from ever being erected again.

Step #3 is to Learn, Believe, and Profess God's Truth. As God reveals to you what doors remain open to the enemy in your mind and thought life, it is incumbent on you to take the time to research His Word and find what He has to say to you on that specific matter. Once you have that truth, write it down, learn it, meditate on it often, and when the enemy tries to get you to believe it about yourself again - speak it out loud, profess what you now believe. You will find the enemy will back down (James 4:7), just as he did when Jesus did the same thing during his temptation.

Other examples of God's truth vs. Satan's lies:

Living in fear - "*God has not given us a spirit of fear, but of power, love and a sound mind*" - 2 Timothy 1:7

Dealing with Anxiety - "*Don't be anxious for anything but in everything, with prayer and supplication, make your request known to God; and the peace of God will keep/guard your heart and mind through Christ Jesus*" - Philippians 4:6.

If you don't know God's Word, you will not have the weapon with which to overcome the lies, accusations and deceptions whispered by the enemy. If you know His Word and don't use it, you are also impotent against the enemy's assault. Satan is not bothered by you owning a Bible and giving it an occasional read. He doesn't get nervous when you have a short "quiet time" in order to check that off your Christian duty box for the day.

What makes him shake in his boots, is a believer who not only reads the Word, but knows and believes the Word and then speaks (professes) the Word aloud in prayer. Remember - Satan and his forces are not omniscient. They cannot read/ hear your thoughts, so speaking the truth of God's Word aloud brandishes the Sword of the Spirit and invokes "divine power" (see 2 Corinthians 10:4) in the spiritual realm.

Knowing and professing God's Word makes us "more than conquerors" in spiritual warfare.

When Jesus was confronted by Satan in the wilderness (Matthew 4:1-11), he spoke. He didn't think about a Bible verse, or silently pray a passage of Scripture - he spoke the Word, and the devil took a hike. We must develop the powerful habit of speaking the Word of God out loud, especially when battling the enemy.

Cleaning out the rat food begins with us identifying and removing all the agreements we have made with the enemy. For most of us, this will take some time to work through, but it will be worth it. As believers, we don't have to be tormented by Satan's schemes or weighed down by his debilitating accusations and lies.

I can't encourage you enough to take the time to identify any and all agreements you may have made in your past, and write them down somewhere. God will help you bring them to light and get rid of them, but you need to take whatever time you need to focus on them.

Agreements from your past also include agreements in the "recent" past, as in yesterday. You will discover that many of your current battles stem from agreements made in your past, even as a child. You may also discover that Satan is currently knocking on a new door, lying to you about a current thought or feeling, and whispering for you to agree with another avenue of deceptive thinking. Ask God to help you identify not only the old wounded thoughts and agreements, but also any new assaults being launched against you.

After you have taken the time to write down what God reveals to you - move on to the next Chapter and let's talk about what else is critical is becoming free and staying free from Satan's influence.

My child, listen to what I say, and treasure my commands.

Tune your ears to wisdom, and concentrate on understanding.

Cry out for insight, and ask for understanding.

Search for them as you would for silver; seek them like hidden treasures.

Then you will understand what it means to fear the Lord,

and you will gain knowledge of God.

For the Lord grants wisdom! From his mouth

come knowledge and understanding.

He grants a treasure of common sense to the honest.

He is a shield to those who walk with integrity.

He guards the paths of the just and protects those who are faithful to him.

Then you will understand what is right, just, and fair,

and you will find the right way to go.

For wisdom will enter your heart, and knowledge will fill you with joy.

Wise choices will watch over you. Understanding will keep you safe.

Wisdom will save you from evil people, from those whose words are twisted.

These men turn from the right way to walk down dark paths.

They take pleasure in doing wrong, and they enjoy the twisted ways of evil.

Their actions are crooked, and their ways are wrong.

Wisdom will save you from the immoral woman, from the

seductive words of the promiscuous woman.

She has abandoned her husband and ignores

the covenant she made before God.

Entering her house leads to death, it is the road to the grave.

The man who visits her is door. He will never reach the paths of life.

So follow the steps of the good, and stay on the paths of the righteous.

For only the godly will live in the land, and those

with integrity will remain in it.

But the wicked will be removed from the land, and the

treacherous will be uprooted.

Proverbs 2

Chapter Nine

Cleaning Your Physical House

Let's begin this discussion by looking at what God says:

Romans 6:6 - *knowing this, that our old man was crucified with Him, that the body of sin might be done away with, that we should no longer be slaves of sin.*

Romans 6:14 - *sin shall not have dominion over you*

Galatians 5:1 - *Stand fast therefore in the liberty by which Christ has made us free, and do not be entangled again with a yoke of bondage.*

Jesus death, and resurrection broke the power that sin has over us. We were born sinners, separated from God, and slaves to sin - but Jesus set us free from that slavery. We still, however, have the choice to "go back to the slavery and bondage of Egypt" sort of speak, by choosing to hang on to our sinful habits and propensities. By doing so, we open wide the doors to our soul for the enemy to freely construct strongholds from which to control our thoughts and lives.

We are probably all familiar with scenarios like - the alcoholic who gets saved and swears off alcohol *forever*. Trouble is, he still keeps alcohol in the house and continues to hang out with buddies who drink regularly and freely. The usual progression is - this well-meaning believer experiences some hard circumstances, or unusual stress, or some triggering event and our ever-present enemy is right there to whisper to him. "You need a drink". "Just one". "God knows what kind of stress you're under, you deserve this, surely He understands".

These dramas play out daily in the lives of Christians everywhere. We swear off an old vice, or habit, that we know we shouldn't do. We are tempted again (by you-know-who) and then justify a reason to pick it back up, feel terrible afterward, are riddled with guilt and shame, and then swear an oath to God that we will *never do it again*.

Notice that these battles begin in our minds. Like Eve, we are tempted by the enemy, and begin to contemplate the "offer". As is usually the case, that contemplation leads to justification, which results in taking action. Anger outbursts, watching pornography, binge eating, binge drinking or spending, gambling, drugs, etc. - all have their roots in our mind.

So, another obvious place where we have to clean house is our physical house. By this, I mean getting rid of the physical triggers and temptations that will eventually call out to us. If you want to lose weight, get in shape and eat right - you have to get rid of the ice cream in your freezer and anything else that you know is going to be a temptation. Desiring to quit smoking/drinking - you've got to throw it all away, stay away from people and places where you will be tempted and don't purchase again.

If you are tempted with lust, infidelity, sensuality, pornography, etc. - you have got to get rid of any apps on your phone, websites on your laptop, and any premium cable channels that temp you with the exact programming you are being drawn to. Get off social media if that is a source of temptation. Delete tempting apps.

Unfriend tempting people. Get an old-fashioned phone that only makes/receives calls. You may need to take drastic action in order to build barriers to protect yourself. I think you get the point.

If you are living in constant fear, yet watch TV, movies and videos filled with violence and horror - don't expect to find freedom from fear. God will not do for you what you need to do for yourself.

Take the time to think and pray through any area in your life where you seem to be consistently losing the battle with temptation. Ask God for wisdom regarding what trash needs to be thrown out in order to begin experiencing more freedom over those areas.

Share your struggle with a trusted friend and have them pray daily for you and hold you accountable.

Getting free and staying free from evil strongholds requires deliberate and continued action on our part. A quick prayer asking God to do it for you is not the answer. Be prepared to wrestle with the enemy as you contemplate your approach and especially as you begin to take steps to throw out the trash that feeds his rats. He will bombard your thoughts and insist that you compromise or give up altogether.

Both steps (physical and mental) are crucial in breaking free from "the yoke of bondage" that has held you for this long. You will lose the battle for your thoughts if you keep those physical temptations around. Ridding yourself of only your physical trash won't make the wrestling match for your thought life go away either. Both mental and physical are crucial.

Chapter Ten

Breaking Agreements

Tearing down emotional strongholds so they no longer dominate your thoughts and actions can come only through an intentional alignment (agreement) of your thoughts with God's truth in the Bible.
– Dr. Tony Evans

Now that you've become familiar with the term "agreement", and have begun writing down those you have made in your past - let's learn how to break them, and their power over you.

Ungodly agreements are false beliefs or inner vows we make during moments of deep hurt, disappointment, failure, fear, anger, or sin. They become internal "contracts" we live by - statements we allow to define our identity, expectations, and behavior.

Many, not all, agreements trace back to:

- Childhood wounds - harsh words or actions, absence, neglect, or even abuse

- Shame from sin - Satan relentlessly reminds, accuses, and shames us

- Trauma - betrayal, abuse, sickness, or death of a loved one, bullying, divorce

- Comparison culture - Satan uses media and culture to further shame us and inflict feelings of inferiority and insecurity

- Unconfessed sin, such as unforgiveness

In his devotional, 30 Days to Overcoming Emotion Strongholds, Dr. Evans also states, " Emotional strongholds come in all shapes and sizes - doubt, fear, poor self-esteem, pride, anxiety, anger, addiction, independence, selfishness, stubbornness, a victim mentality, unforgiveness, and defeatism".

Now that you have taken the time to identify one or more lies from your past, you need to honestly assess if you have made any agreements with those lies, no matter how small or insignificant it may seem or how long ago spoken. If God brought it to your mind, it is significant.

The following is a process for wrestling each of those agreements to the ground and declaring victory over them. While it may appear too simplistic, as children of the King of Kings, "seated with Him in heavenly places", endowed with "authority over all the power of the evil one" in Jesus - this is not simplistic at all.

It cost Jesus his life. Because of Him, we have been given the right and authority to use "divinely powerful weapons" in our battle with the evil one, and be victorious.

This process takes the form of both a verbal confession to God, a verbal renunciation to the forces responsible for the lie in the first place, and a verbal proclamation of your freedom from it. We will begin in this Chapter and continue in the final Chapter.

#1 - Acknowledge & Renounce - Think of this process as a prayer, <u>spoken aloud</u> to God, that is also heard in the spiritual realm by Satan and his forces of darkness. In doing this, you are confessing and renouncing your unholy agreement with the enemy to God and declaring to the enemy that you are "officially" tearing up the contract (agreement) you made with him by doing so.

In my example earlier, this would look like:

> Father, I ask You to forgive me for believing Satan's lie that I am not good enough and that I am doomed to be a failure all of my life. I confess that as sin, and I choose today to believe only what You say about me as the truth. I am Your beloved son, and so valuable to You that You sent Jesus to die in my place. I renounce Satan's lie that I am doomed to be a failure in my life pursuits, and declare that I am not a failure. I am God's son; deeply loved by You: I am royalty; a joint heir with Jesus of His heavenly kingdom. I am more than enough; I can do all things through Christ who strengthens me; The Spirit of God lives in me and is guiding me into the "good plans" You have prepared for me. In the powerful name of Jesus, and by the authority I have been given by Him, I renounce any agreement I have made with failure, inadequacy and inferiority - and declare that I am set free from them today.

This prayer need not be loud and melodramatic, but simply spoken with conviction and honesty. God hears it, and Satan and his forces hear it. It is powerful and effective in the spiritual realm. Note: it will not make Satan and his minions happy either. You can expect a ramping up of follow-up thoughts like - "that didn't do anything", "you don't really believe that", "you didn't do that right", etc.

Once again - don't give that lie a moment's consideration - reject the lie - thank God for the power and truth of His Word, and move on. I believe the main reason I struggled with my "rats" for so long, was that I didn't know to do this.

If you are like me, you will have to repeat this process multiple times to cover the many doors left open in your soul because of the agreements you have made. There is no hurry. Take your time and trust in God's power and healing.

Satan will knock on those same doors again, hoping you will once again open them and allow him back in. Be on guard. You can't keep him from knocking, but only you can choose not to open the door.

A more in-depth prayer is offered in **Appendix B**. Most strongholds are built with various types of "bricks". In this example of dealing with a spirit of fear, we must realize there are multiple types of fear. It is powerful to uncover and renounce any specific fears you struggle with and not just the blanket category of fear.

Ask God to also reveal to you any other types/forms of the lie you are dealing with. If anxiety, ask what your anxious about and/or what is making you anxious. If alcohol, what is it that draws you to drink it, and what is the effect you are seeking from it? Questions like these can further illuminate other lies associated with your agreement.

What must happen next in order to lock the doors for good and continue to demolish any stronghold(s) Satan has erected in your mind in years past?

Chapter Eleven

The Great Exchange

As a teenager, Michael Jordan was cut from his high school varsity basketball team. At the time, he was devastated. He went home, locked himself in his room, and cried. But instead of giving in to self-doubt, Jordan made a conscious decision: he would use the disappointment as fuel. He replaced the thought "I'm not good enough" with "I'll work until they can't ignore me."

From that day on, his life would change for the better. He trained harder than ever — arriving at the gym early, staying late, and pushing his limits daily. Throughout his career, he maintained a mindset that focused on belief, focus, and learning from failure. One of his most famous quotes captures this mental shift: "I've missed more than 9,000 shots in my career. I've lost almost 300 games… I've failed over and over and over again in my life. And that is why I succeed."

Jordan learned that having the thought that he was a failure didn't make it a reality (unless he agreed with it). A thought was only a thought, not a prophecy. He made a choice that day to reject such thoughts and committed to a disciplined course of action that would set him up for success instead. Even though he (like the rest of us) failed numerous times along the way - those failures on the basketball court didn't make him a failure as a person or a player. They actually propelled him forward with greater resolve and purpose.

#2 - Replace Lies with The Truth - Michael Jordan missed thousands of shots in his career. He committed fouls, made errant passes, got the ball stolen from him, and missed defensive assignments - but he was not a failure. In fact, history will record that he was probably the best basketball player to ever play the game.

If he had made an agreement with the lie that he was a failure when he made mistakes on the court - we might not even know his name today. He could have easily given up on basketball and pursued other, less difficult paths. But he didn't.

What about you?

What debilitating lie or accusation from your youth (or even later) have you uncovered that you have made an agreement with? There is probably at least one, if not many, that you have been carrying around for years. I had strongholds for years that I didn't realize I had allowed to be built.

God continued to reveal others to me, so that I could get free from their gravitational pull:

You'll never be able to ... (be aware of words like "never" and "always") You're father didn't love you.

You're stupid. You'll never get it. God can't forgive you for ... God is mad at you.

Hopefully, by now you have your list and are working on Step #1 for each of them. As Michael Jordan would tell you - now comes the hard work.

Now is the time to go through each lie on your list and research what God says is the truth about it. What does God's Word say about your worth, your intelligence, His forgiveness, etc? This is the ongoing process of replacing Satan's lies with God's Truth - the beginning of "demolishing strongholds". Tearing down strongholds takes hard work, effort, and determination.

I would strongly encourage you to write all this down. Grab a notebook or laptop and write down the lie, and then the Truth next to it. If there are multiple Scriptures pertaining to your stronghold, write them all down.

I assure you that Satan is not going to back down from trying to get you to believe His lies, steal your peace, destroy your joy, and derail your Christian walk. When he comes to that door in your mind again and whispers… you will now have a resource to draw from to gain the upper hand immediately. This is what God intended when He gave us His Word as a weapon, a sword, with which to prevail over the mental/emotional/physical attacks of our enemy.

Let me remind you that these are battles (the Bible calls them "wrestling" matches in Ephesians 6:12), that are yours to fight. Don't pray "God, please take these thoughts away", or "help me not think these thoughts". He gave His children armor, powerful weapons, the Divine power of His name, along with the spiritual authority to use all of them - to engage the enemy every time and triumph. I will also remind you that knowing this is not enough. If you don't DO it, you will continue to walk in bondage to a very cruel master.

Now that you know these things, God will bless you for doing them - John 13:17

Everyone then who hears these words of mine and does them will be like a wise man who built his house on a rock …" - Matthew 7:24-27

Another huge benefit of writing down what God says about the areas of bondage you and I struggle with, is the more you use His sword (Word) in battle, the more familiar you will become with His Word - to the point that at some point down the road, you won't have to look in your notebook for the Scripture. You can pull the Sword out of your own sheath because you have memorized what the Bible says in response to the enemy's lies. You have replaced them with the Truth.

Remember - the only power Satan has over you is the power you allow him to have. Jesus defeated him at the cross (Colossians 2:14-15), disarmed him (Colossians 2:15), and gave us (His children) authority over "all the power of the evil one" (Luke 10:19). We no longer have to believe any accusation or lie he throws our way. The only weapon Satan has, is his mouth. We have to train ourselves to stop listening to his poisonous lies, accusations and deceptions, and only listen to our Father's truthful, powerful, loving words.

#3 - Shut the Doors, and Lock Them - armed with God's Word and authority, we can now shut every door that we have allowed to remain open to Satan's poison, and lock them tightly. The Bible describes this process this way:

"For though we walk in the flesh, we are not waging war according to the flesh. For the weapons of our warfare are not of the flesh but have divine power to destroy strongholds. We destroy arguments and every lofty opinion raised against the knowledge of God, and take every thought captive to obey Christ."
2 Corinthians 10:3-5

When Satan was tempting Eve in Genesis 3, she opened the door to the enemy's deceitful whispers and took time to ponder his "argument". She considered his "opinion" and finally made an agreement with it. That agreement is what led to her action, which was taking a bite of the fruit she had been told not to eat.

When Satan was tempting Jesus in Matthew 4, he heard the enemy's lying arguments and opinions, but instead of giving them a moment's consideration, he "took them captive" and immediately responded with the truth and power of God's Word. He "waged war" with the weapon of Truth, the Sword of the Spirit - God's Word. This sword is our weapon that wields "divine power to destroy strongholds".

It should be obvious then, that if we don't know it, we can't wield it - and if we don't wield it in "our warfare", we remain powerless against the enemy.

Like Jesus, we have the authority to approach every temptation with the divinely powerful Word of God. The same is true in approaching every stronghold that has been erected over time in our minds. When Satan whispers for you to re-open the door of fear, or anxiety, or lust, or whatever you just took the time to identify and renounce, your counterattack with God's Word will send him packing.

You will have chipped a piece of his stronghold away and taken another big step in demolishing it altogether. This is what God tells us to do in James 4:7 - *"Resist the devil, and he will flee from you"*. He doesn't say the devil "might" flee - according to the truth of God's Word, he WILL flee. The opposite, then, is also true. If we do NOT resist him (his lies, deceptions, and accusations), he will NOT flee, but continue to torment us.

Think of "resisting" as the same process Jesus used when tempted - 1. give no place (consideration) to Satan's lying, deceiving thought. - 2. verbally confront him with the appropriate Word of God, and then - 3. tell Him (by the authority given you as God's child) to "be gone" or "flee".

Even though Satan will flee, according to God's Word, he will keep trying.

When the devil had finished every temptation, he [temporarily]
left Him until a more opportune time.
– Luke 4:13 (Amplified).

He is determined to keep you in bondage to his lies, stealing your joy, your witness, and your abundant life. That is why we are also reminded in Scripture to:

Be alert and of sober mind. Your enemy, the devil, prowls around like a roaring
lion looking for someone to devour. Resist him, standing firm in the faith
– 1 Peter 5:8-9

Put on the full armor of God, so that you can take
your stand against the devil's schemes.
– Ephesians 6:11

For we wrestle not against flesh and blood, but against principalities,
against powers, against the rulers of the darkness of this world,
against spiritual wickedness in high places.
– Ephesians 6:12

Here is where the "wrestling" (Greek = "hand to hand combat", "struggle") takes place. Satan is relentless. He is determined. He will return. When he does, we must "wrestle" with him in our thought life. In the battlefield of our mind, we must stay alert, on guard, dressed for battle, hand on our Sword - ready to do exactly what Jesus did. Recognize the lie and rebut it with the Truth. If you have ever wrestled, or talked with anyone who has competed as a wrestler, they will tell you that in a contest you can not relax or ease up for a second or your opponent will take advantage and gain control.

That is why we read the Bible. We are at war. Any reason to read the Bible is a good one, but to simply read it to complete your One Year Reading Plan, or to feel that you are doing your duty as a good Christian man or woman, is not the goal.

The goal is to live victoriously over a mortal enemy who wishes to "devour" (utterly destroy) us.

Satan's greatest weapon is man's ignorance of God's Word.
A.W. Tozer

The Word of God is the sword with which the devil is
driven away and his schemes are destroyed.
John Calvin

A house without Scripture is like a city without walls.
John Chrysostom

This is how we keep the enemy out of our heads and demolish any existing stronghold(s) from our past. They were erected brick by brick, lie by lie, agreement by agreement - and we must bring them down by continuing to renounce the lies and profess the Truth.

#4 - Change Your Mind - it should be obvious by now that continuing to supply food to the "rats" in your mind will only serve to keep them fat and happy right where they are. What we are encouraged and implored to do in Scripture is to begin the ongoing discipline of changing our mind./thoughts.

- *Do not be conformed to this present world, but be transformed by the renewing of your mind* - Romans 12:2a

- *Put off the old self...and be renewed in the spirit of your mind* - Ephesians 4:22

- *Set your minds on things that are above, not on things that are on earth* - Colossians 3:2

- *The mind set on the flesh is death, but the mind set on the spirit is life and peace* - Romans 8:6

- *Finally, brothers and sisters, whatever is true, whatever is worthy of respect, whatever is just, whatever is pure, whatever is lovely, whatever is commendable, if something is excellent or praiseworthy, think about these things* - Philippians 4:8

The only way a stronghold can be demolished is for us to continue to wrestle against Satan's ongoing assault on our minds. Each time we resist his knock on the door (the lie, deception, or accusation) with the powerful truth of God - the stronghold crumbles further. The more it crumbles, the more freedom we experience.

The acts of "not conforming", "putting off", "setting your minds", and "thinking about" - all rest with us. They are incumbent on us. We are the only ones who can change our thought patterns and do what God says needs to be done to transform our minds, our thoughts, emotions, and actions. Only then will we experience the freedom He has promised and the joy that accompanies it.

Thankfully, God promises His help in our struggle:

> Isaiah 41:10 - *fear not, for I am with you; be not dismayed, for I am your God. I will strengthen you, I will help you, I will uphold you with my righteous right hand.*

> Philippians 2:13 - *for it is God who works in you, both to will and to work for his good pleasure.*

> Philippians 4:13 - *I can do all this through him who gives me strength.*

> Ephesians 6:10 - *Finally, be strong in the Lord and in the strength of his might.*

> 2 Corinthians 10:4 - *For the weapons of our warfare are not of the flesh but have divine power to destroy strongholds.*

Take Out the Trash

A top priority in this discipline is - getting rid of the rat food. The enemy will capitalize, and we will most likely compromise, if all the trash is not taking away and destroyed.

Like many middle-aged men, I put on a few extra pounds over the years and thought often about shedding those ponds and "getting back in shape". A couple of years ago, I finally decided to "do" what I knew was the right thing to do. My wife and I joined a local athletic club very close to our home and committed to go daily. Because we were paying a monthly membership, we felt more obliged to go so we weren't wasting our money.

Everyone knows by now that if you want to lose weight and get in shape, you need to throw out the junk food, the high-calorie, empty-calorie food, and begin to eat a healthy, nutritious diet. After replacing the bad with good, you need to get off the sofa and move - exercise, burn calories, and discipline yourself to do what it takes to get the results you want. We all also know that all of those things are difficult to do. I love my bread, pasta, rice, fried chicken, ice cream, homemade cookies, etc..

There is no easy way to achieve the results you want, so the choice for us was to start slow, and "just go". Watching other "older" people walking, lifting and cycling was actually motivating. What was even more motivating was feeling and looking better in just a matter of weeks. Now, the discipline we were reluctant to begin is a habit we can't seem to do without. We are reaping the rewards of sowing.

The same is true when it comes to "re-wiring" our thought life. Yes, it is difficult at first, and takes discipline. Like exercise, the more you do it, the better you get at it, and the more you enjoy the benefits. We need to start by "getting off the spiritual couch" sort of speak. The hardest step is the first one. Just start, and trust God to bless your journey.

As much as possible, try to avoid situations, media, and people that invite negative, destructive thoughts to come knocking. If you struggle with a fear of harm, or even death - stop watching media that portrays the very thing you are fearful of. Keep it out of your mind. If you want to clean up your vulgar thought life and language habit - quit listening to music filled with vulgar, suggestive, and demonic language.

Many men today, and a growing number of women, struggle with sexual sin. All sexual sin begins in the mind, so once again, it only makes sense to examine the sources of your thoughts. Are you feeding those rats with sexually explicit television, movies, music, internet, social media, etc.? The rats will not leave as long as you keep feeding them.

Changing your mind and your thought patterns takes work. It takes sacrifice. It takes discipline.

The difficulty we run into is this - our flesh actually likes flirting with and indulging in our old ways of thinking and acting. We want to lose the weight, but we don't want to give up the foods we love. We want to quit drinking, but we enjoy the escape after a long day at the office. We're ashamed of our lustful or adulterous thoughts, but we secretly enjoy the rush from watching things we know we shouldn't.

I have often said in marriage counseling situations with couples - "people do what they <u>really</u> want to do". Michael Jordan changed his thoughts and put in hours and hours of hard work to achieve his dream because he really, really wanted it. Even when he failed to make the game-winning basket, he got back in the gym and kept working.

So, what is the #1 thing you are struggling with today? Is there a spiritual stronghold of unforgiveness, anger, anxiety, unconfessed sin, depression, discouragement, fear, lust, addiction, spiritual apathy, etc.?

As believers, God has given us all the tools we need to demolish every existing stronghold in our minds. We also have the authority to use those tools to exact the changes we desire, and the freedom that results.

But - do we <u>really</u> want it bad enough to do what it takes to achieve it? Only you can answer that one.

Chapter Twelve
Get Up,
Keep Running

1 Corinthians 9:24-27, "*Do you not know that in a race all the runners run, but only one receives the prize? So run that you may obtain it.*

2 Timothy 4:7-8, *"I have fought the good fight, I have finished the race, I have kept the faith.*

At the 1972 Munich Olympics, Finnish runner Lasse Virén tripped and fell to the track halfway through the grueling 10,000 meter final. He watched in shock as the entire pack of runners passed him by. What thoughts can you imagine were flooding through his mind in that moment? "what's the use?", "you've lost, don't even try", "don't embarrass yourself", are a few options that come to mind. What would you have done? What did Lasse do?

He scrambled to his feet and regained his rhythm. Not only did he catch the other runners, he won the Olympic gold medal while setting a new world record.

We all fall from time to time. Michael Jordan missed key shots that lost his team games and pro baseball players typically get out much more than they get hits. All Christians stumble and fall. When that happens, be assured our enemy will be immediately at the door knocking. You will hear him accuse you, demean you, shame you - "you did that again!", "you're probably not even saved", "God is so disappointed in you", "you'll never change", and many more.

The pattern is this:

- We fall (sin).

- Satan immediately brings guilt and shame.

- The Spirit brings conviction and Godly sorrow.

- Satan seeks to convince you that you are an utter failure, a hypocrite and a disappointment to God. "It's best to just give up, you'll never change".

- The Spirit seeks to convict you of your sin, bring you to repent and ask God's forgiveness.

- God promises to forgive your sin, cleanse you, and restore fellowship with you.

- You decide whether to get up and run, or sit on the track believing you are a failure.

Abraham fell. Moses fell. David fell. Peter fell. We all fall. (Romans 3:10, Psalm 14:2-3)

But, when you fall, you need to a) acknowledge your failure (confess), b) ask for God's forgiveness, and, (c) based on the truth of Scripture (1 John 1:9) **get up, dust yourself off, and get back in the race.** The Bible calls us to "repent" - which basically means to "turn around and walk away from your sinful thinking and way of life".

Luke 5:32
I have not come to call the righteous, but sinners to repentance."

Acts 3:19
Repent, then, and turn to God, so that your sins may be wiped out, that times of refreshing may come from the Lord,

Acts 8:22
Repent of this wickedness and pray to the Lord in the hope that he may forgive you for having such a thought in your heart.

2 Corinthians 7:10
Godly sorrow brings repentance that leads to salvation and leaves no regret, but worldly sorrow brings death.

<u>2 Peter 3:9</u>

The Lord is not slow in keeping his promise, as some understand slowness. Instead he is patient with you, not wanting anyone to perish, but everyone to come to repentance.

Do not allow the enemy any room in your head, but resist his accusations and condemnation. Thank the Lord that you can confess your sin to Him, and ask Him, once again, to cleanse and forgive you. His promise is that He will not only forgive your sin, but separate you from them "as far as East is from West" (Psalm 103:12).

While repentance is an amazing gift from our Father, we must also humbly remember that our grace to repent of our sin and be cleansed from it, cost Jesus his life. He volunteered to leave His magnificent throne in heaven to come to earth, be tempted in every way like we are, be unjustly arrested, brutally beaten, and suffer the agony of crucifixion at the hands of the humans He had lovingly created.

Our sin put Jesus on the cross, and every time we willingly sin again, we show our ungratefulness for His suffering and betray His love for us.

Chapter Thirteen
Developing Your Strategy

Guard your heart above all else, for it determines the course of your life.
– Proverbs 4:23

Have you ever given a moments thought to what that verse actually means? What does it look like to "guard our heart/mind"? Do you and I have a strategy in place to do that? Is it really that necessary?

I would conclude that if guarding our heart/mind "*determines the course of our life*", it may need to become a top priority.

Hopefully, you now have the components by which to develop such a strategy. Let me take a minute to recap and outline those components so you will have them all on one place.

1. Make time to get alone with God, notebook in hand, and ask Him to meet with you and speak with you about your heart and the ways Satan may have influenced your thinking (and actions) in the past.

2. Ask God to shine His light on any wounds (people, words, actions, events, etc.) from your past that have negatively impacted you. What do you think about yourself? What do others think about you? What does God think about you? Ask Him to touch any hurtful place in your life and bring it to your mind. Write them down.

3. Ask yourself, and God, whether you made an agreement with one or more of those things. Did you take the enemy's lie, deception, accusation, etc. and made it personal - I AM that thing. Write those down also. This is key, because those agreements are what allowed Satan permission to come setup camp in your mind and begin building strongholds.

4. Are there any current wounds that have formed or you know are forming that are causing you anxiety, fear, depression, loneliness, unforgiveness, etc. Write these down as well.

5. Take whatever time needed to search the Scriptures to find what God's Word says about your agreement, or the lie Satan has been, or is, speaking to you.

   If you can't locate one, ask a mature believer to help you find what God says. This is where you need to write God's truth beside the lie/agreement that you have believed.

6. Take the time with each hurt/wound/agreement to confess your acknowledgment to God (out loud) and ask Him to forgive you for believing a lie and agreeing with it. Then, renounce (out loud) each of those agreements to Satan and his forces and acknowledge that by the power of Jesus' blood and His name, you are breaking your agreement and choosing to believe God's truth. Tell him he is no longer welcome in your mind, and that you are resisting him in Jesus name - then command that he leave.

7. You have gotten your heart right with God and begun tearing down the enemy's fortress/influence in your mind. According to Scripture, he must flee, but remember, he will attempt to get you to reconsider your decision and re-open a door once again. This is where we must learn to walk daily in God's Word, and ask the Spirit to alert you to the enemy's presence. The Spirit's power is critical in helping you discern whether your thoughts are from God, or from the enemy. Remember 2 Corinthians 10:3-5 and Hebrews 5:14.

8. Begin to clean your physical house of people, places and things that will attract the rats and entice them to return. The Bible reminds us to "put off", to "put on", to "clothe yourself", etc. - and that is a daily discipline of immersing yourself in God's Word and in personal prayer.

9. Determine to get back up and keep running when you fall. Acknowledge your sin, ask for His forgiveness, and do not listen to the enemy's condemning voice.

10. Ask a believing friend and/or mentor to run with you.

"For though we walk in the flesh, we are not waging war according to the flesh. For the weapons of our warfare are not of the flesh but have divine power to destroy strongholds. We destroy arguments and every lofty opinion raised against the knowledge of God, and take every thought captive to obey Christ."

2 Corinthians 10:3-5

While Satan has control over the great majority of the people, events and culture of the world around us - we will be focusing on his schemes to derail, distract and destroy those of us who call ourselves Christians.

The only thing that gives Satan more pleasure than keeping people from the light and life of the gospel of Christ - is wreaking havoc in the lives of God's beloved people.

He cannot "un-save" a believer, but he can get us so distracted by the worries of this life, the frantic pace of raising a family, the relentless pursuit of wealth and leisure, the emotional crippling of worry, fear, anxiety, addiction and despair - and so many other things - that our lives are anything but "abundant" and filled with love, joy, peace and kingdom fruit - not to mention making Him known to the hordes of spiritually lost and dying people all around us.

We can't settle for an infrequent and tertiary "quiet time" with God, and have no knowledge of the power given to us in the sword of the Spirit. We know the verse, but fail to practice "taking every thought captive to make it obedient to Christ" because we don't understand the way Satan works on our minds and the strongholds we allow him to build there.

We can no longer settle for being ill-equipped in our spiritual, emotional and physical struggles against Satan and his forces of darkness. It is high time to walk as children of the King and enforce the spiritual authority we have been granted over our enemy.

With God's help, it is time we closed all the doors Satan uses as access points into our mind, and walk in victory over the enemy of our soul.

Now, let's get to work.

Appendix A

Who Am I in Christ?

I Am Accepted in Christ

John 1:12	I am a child of God
John 10:27-30	I am His sheep and He knows me personally
John 15:15	I am Christ's friend
John 15:16	He chose me and appointed me to bear fruit
Romans 5:1	I have been justified and sanctified in Christ
Romans 8:28-30	I am called according to His purpose
I Cor. 6:20	I have been bought with a price: I belong to God
I Cor. 8:3	I am known by God
I Cor. 12:27	I am a member of Christ's Body
Gal. 4:4-7	I am a child of God and also an heir
Eph. 1:1	I am a saint
Eph. 1:5	I have been adopted as God's child
Eph. 2:18	I have direct access to God through the Holy Spirit
Col. 1:14	I have been redeemed and forgiven of all my sins
Col. 2:10	I am complete in Christ

I Am Secure in Christ

Luke 10:18	My name is written in heaven
Romans 4:7-8	My sins have completely and permanently forgiven
Romans 5:1-2	I have peace with God
Romans 6:18	I have been set free from the law of sin
Romans 8:1,2	I am forever free from condemnation
Romans 8:28	I am assured that all things work together for my good

Romans 8:35	I cannot be separated from the love of God
I Cor. 3:16	God's Spirit lives in me
2 Cor. 1:21	I have been established, anointed and sealed by God
Gal. 2:20	Christ lives in me
Gal. 5:1	Christ has set me free from Satan's bondage
Eph. 2:1-10	I am seated with Christ, far above Satan's dominion
Phil. 1:6	I know God will perfect the good work He has begun in me
Phil. 3:20	I am a citizen of heaven
2 Tim. 1:7	I don't have a spirit of fear, but of power, love & a sound mind
Heb. 4:16	I can always come before Him to find grace and mercy in time of need

Other Books by Rob Thorpe

VICTORIOUS
Winning the Spiritual Battles in Your Life

Hand Me Downs
What to do About Generational Iniquity

All In
A Marriage Worth Dying For

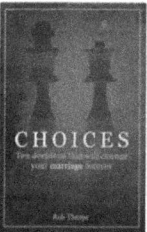

CHOICES
10 Decisions That Will Change
Your Marriage Forever

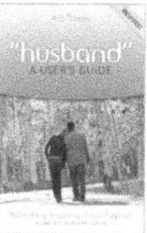

"husband" - A User's Guide

Next Steps
Beginning Your New Life in Christ

www.ingramcontent.com/pod-product-compliance
Lightning Source LLC
Chambersburg PA
CBHW081636040426
42449CB00014B/3336